I0464875

EASY ANI-MANDALA COLORING BOOK

For

Grandma

© 2015 Argon Media LLC

All Rights reserved. No part of this book may be reproduced or used in any way or form or by any means whether electronic or mechanical, this means that you cannot record or photocopy any material ideas or tips that are provided in this book.

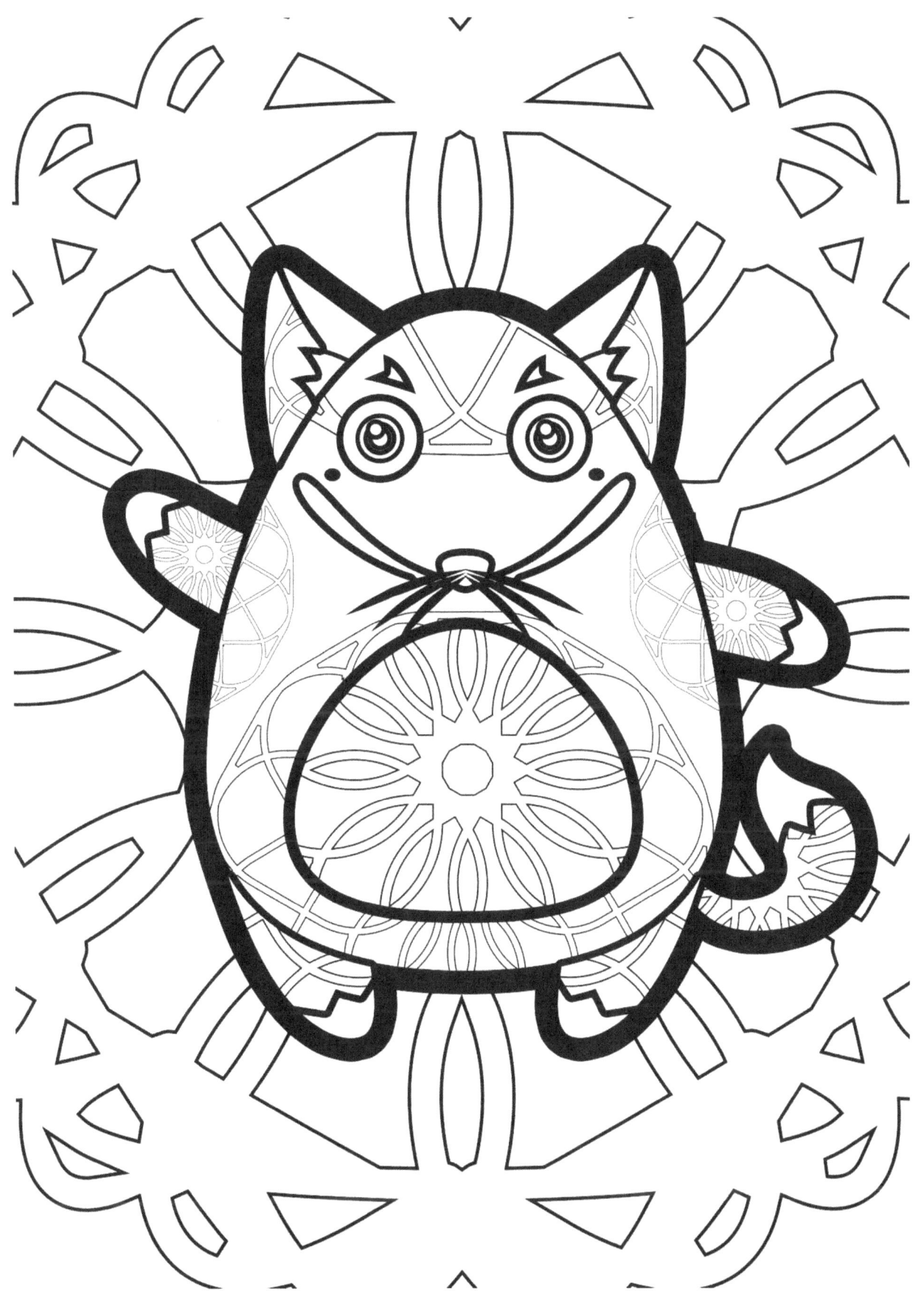

This is a Bleed Through Page If You Are Using a Coloring Marker or Pen!

Find Other Great Titles By Us. Search on Your Favorite Book Retailer.

Amazon.com | Barens & Noble (BN.Com) | Books A Million (BAM.com)

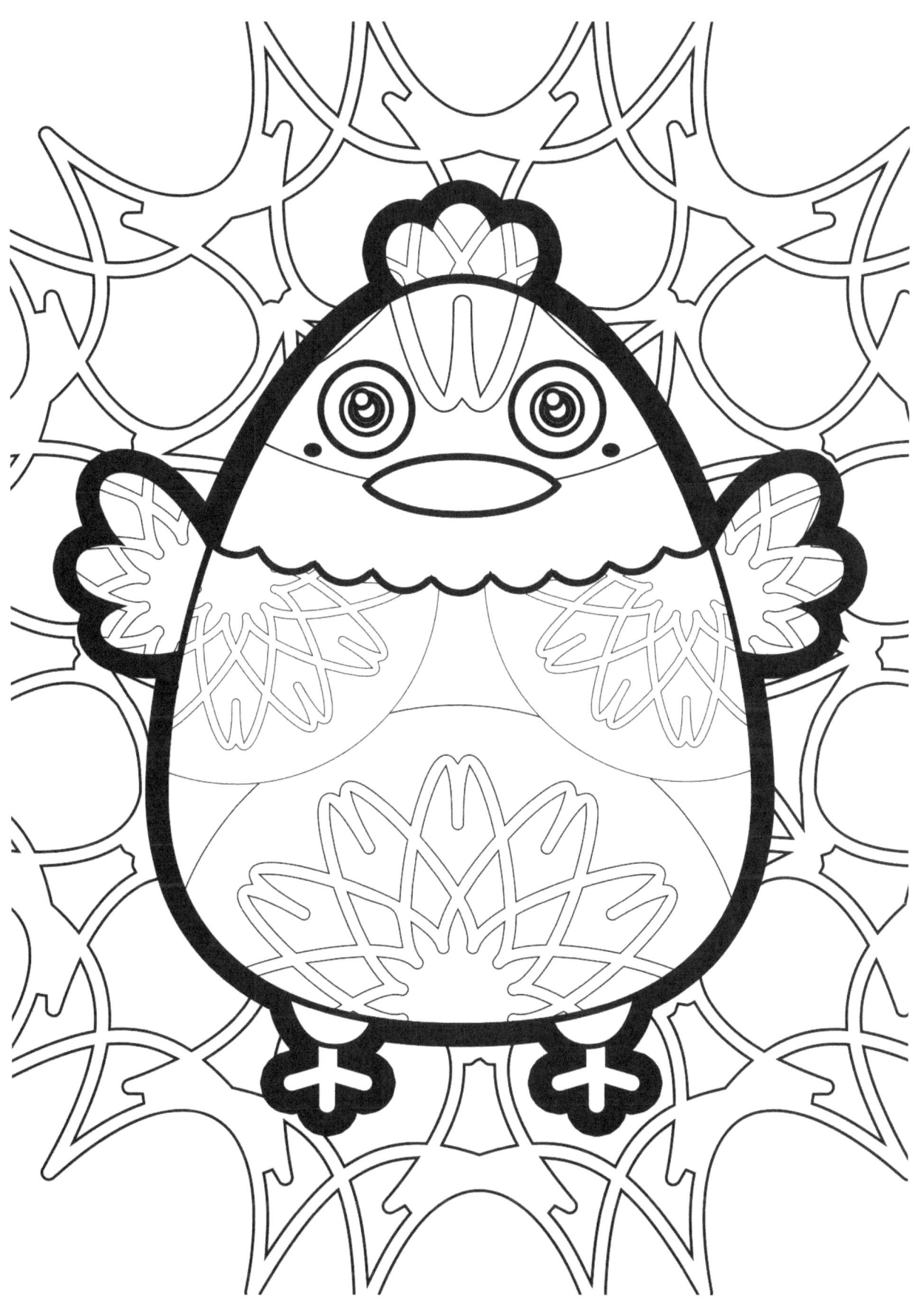

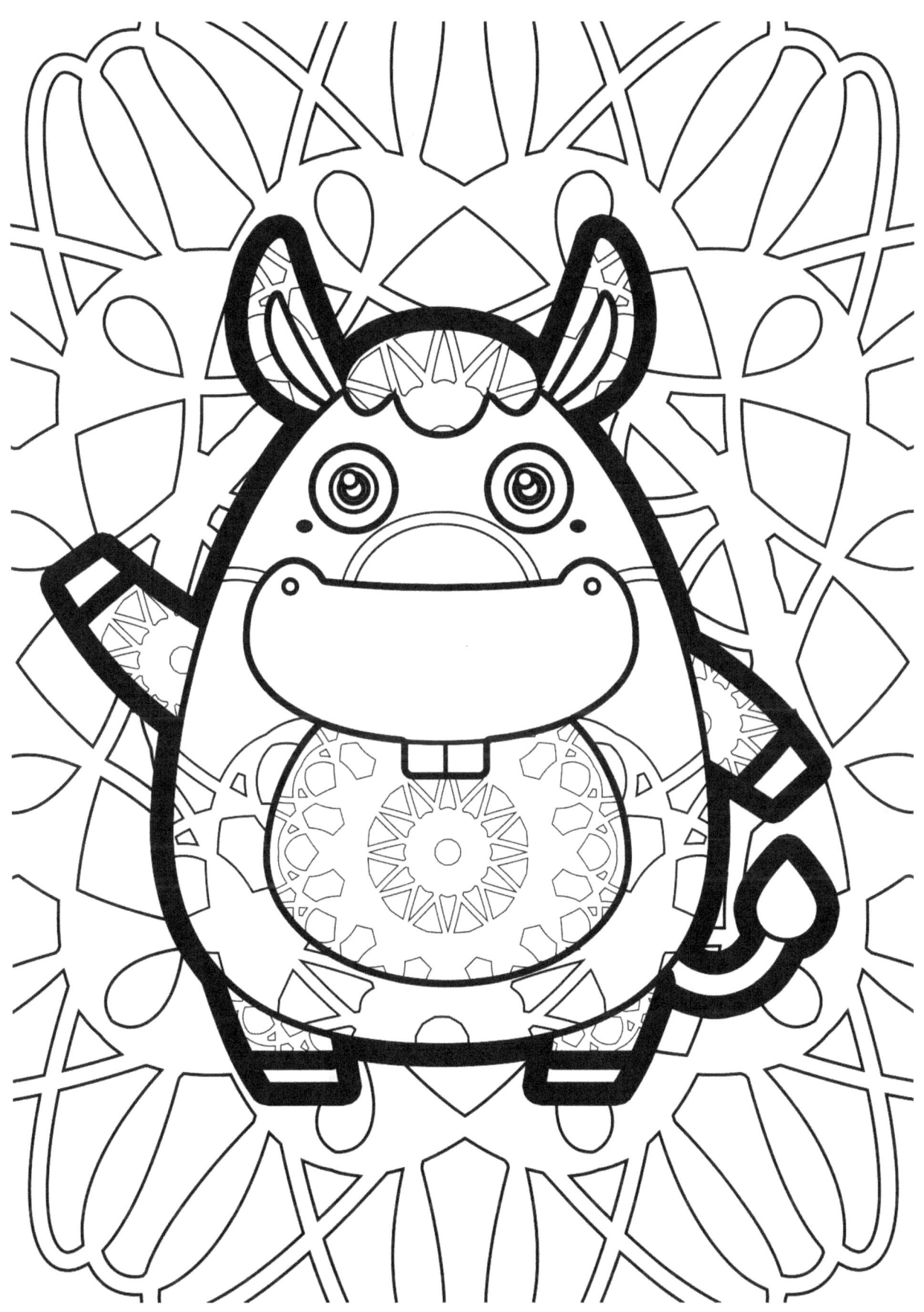

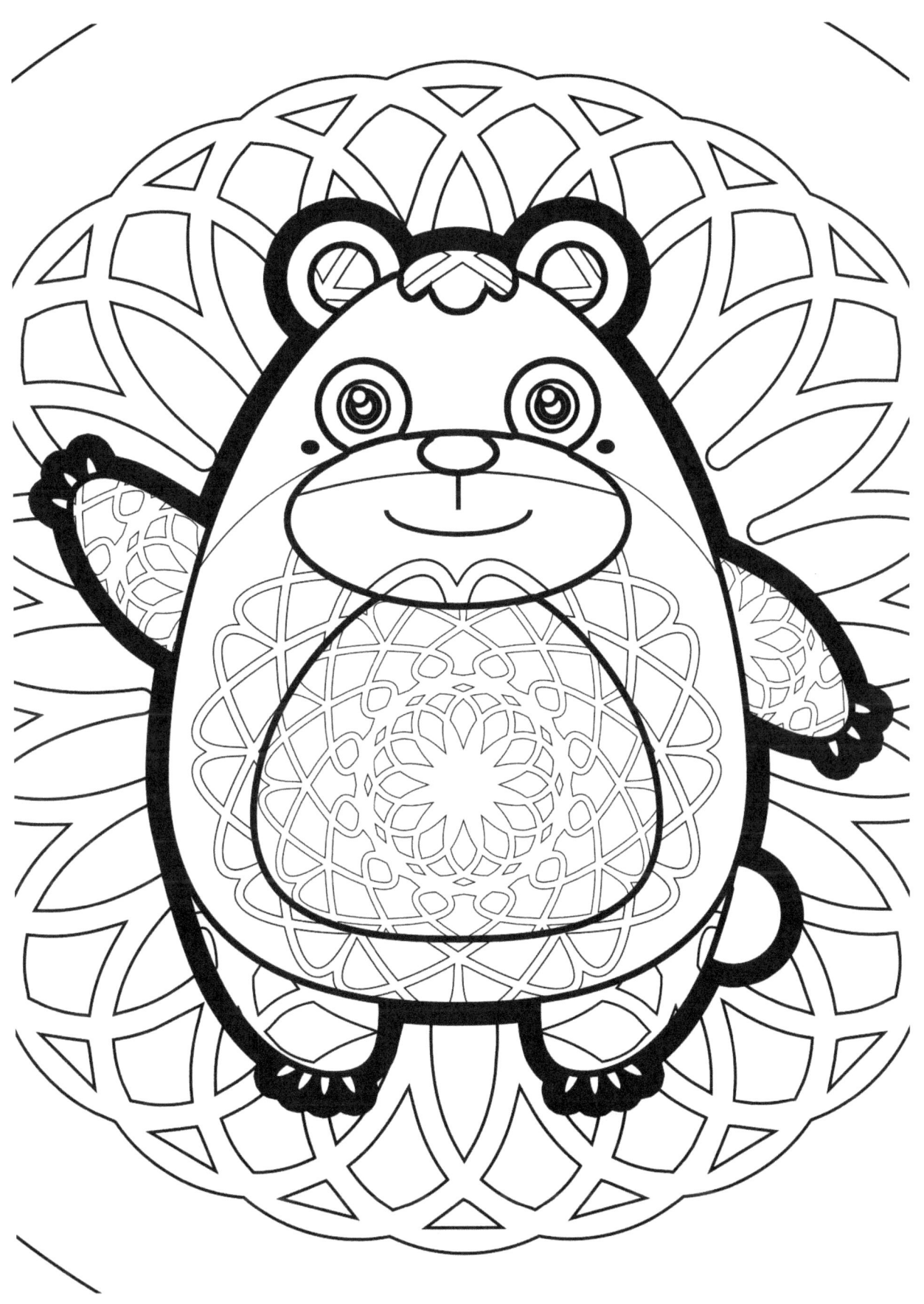

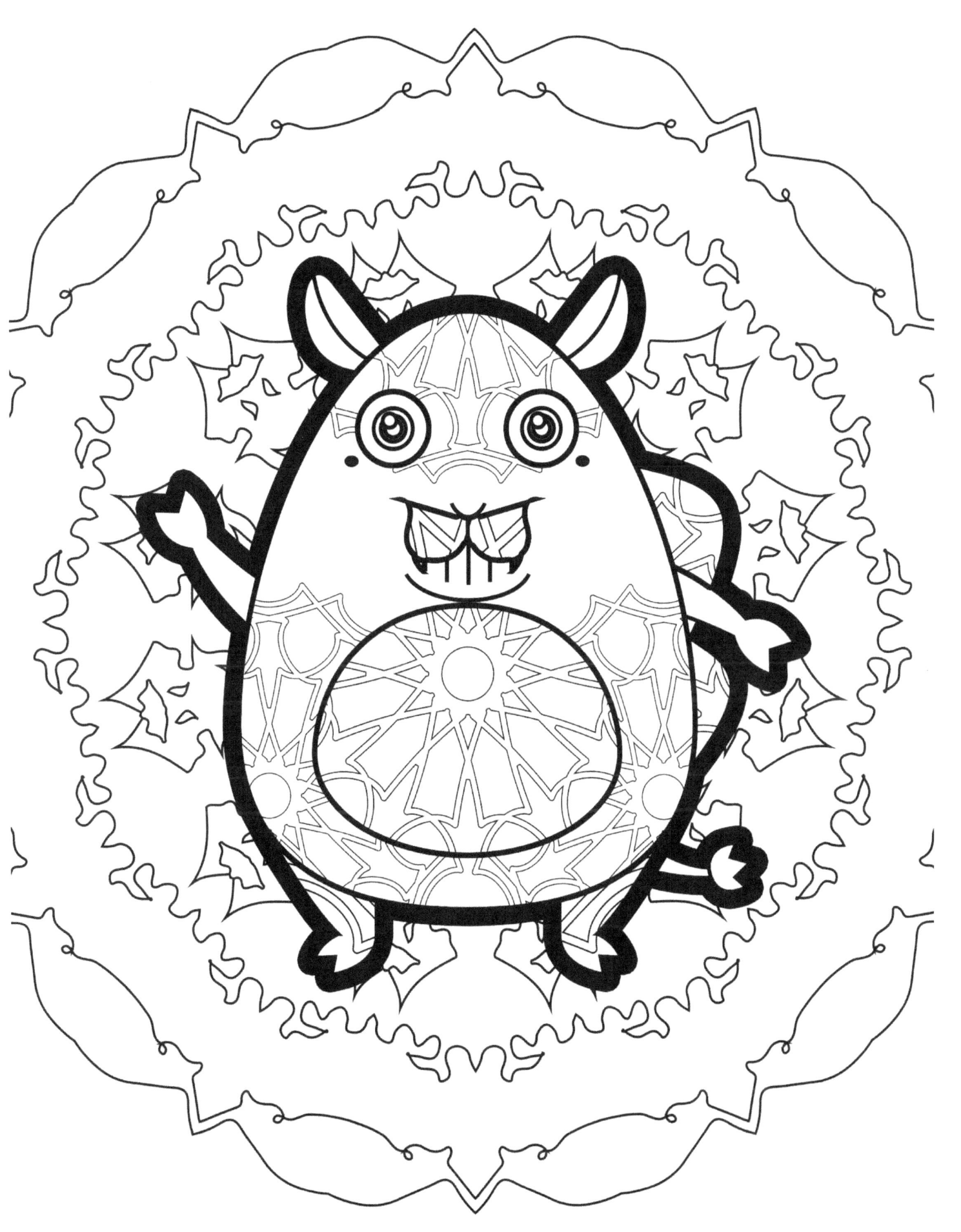

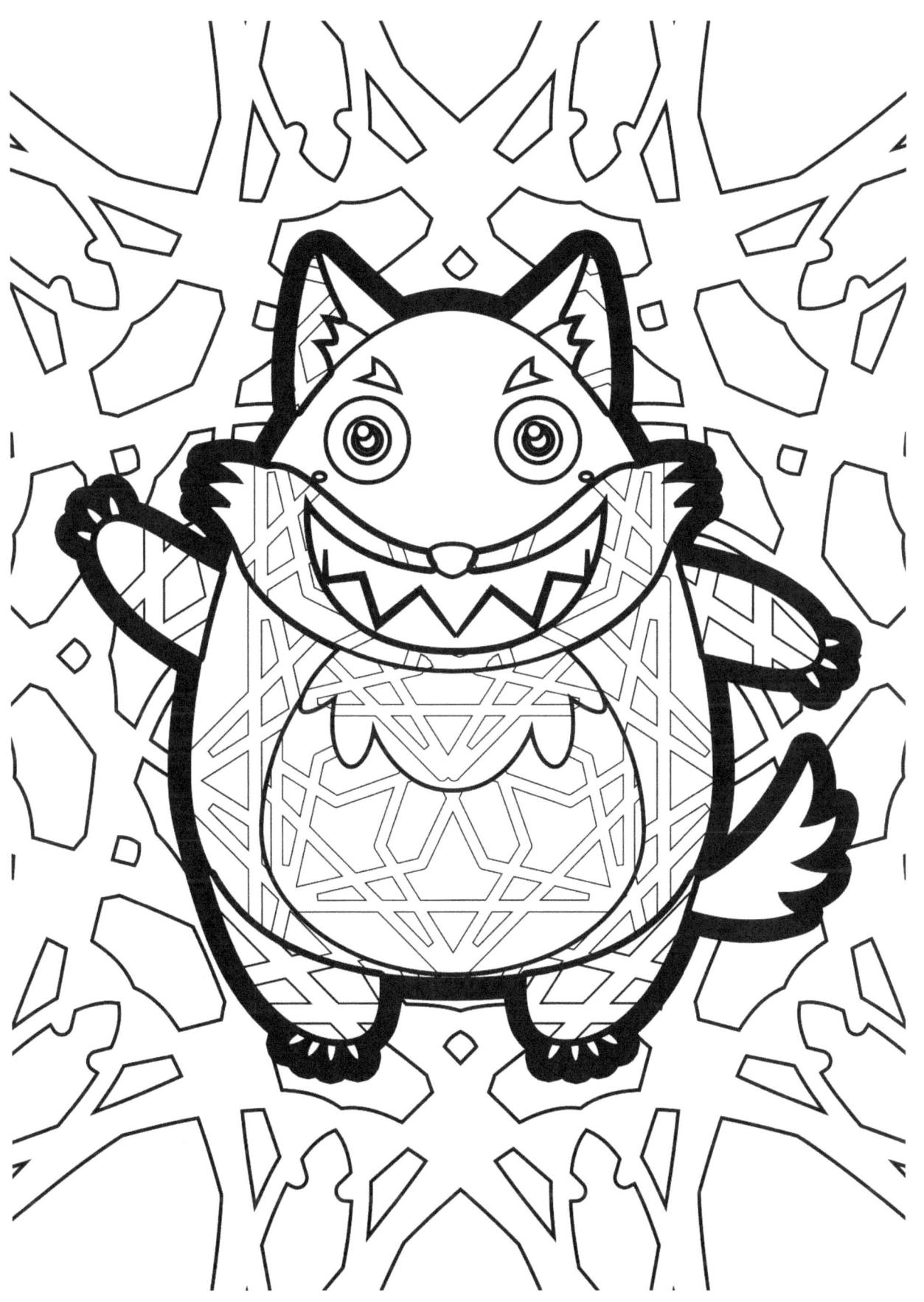

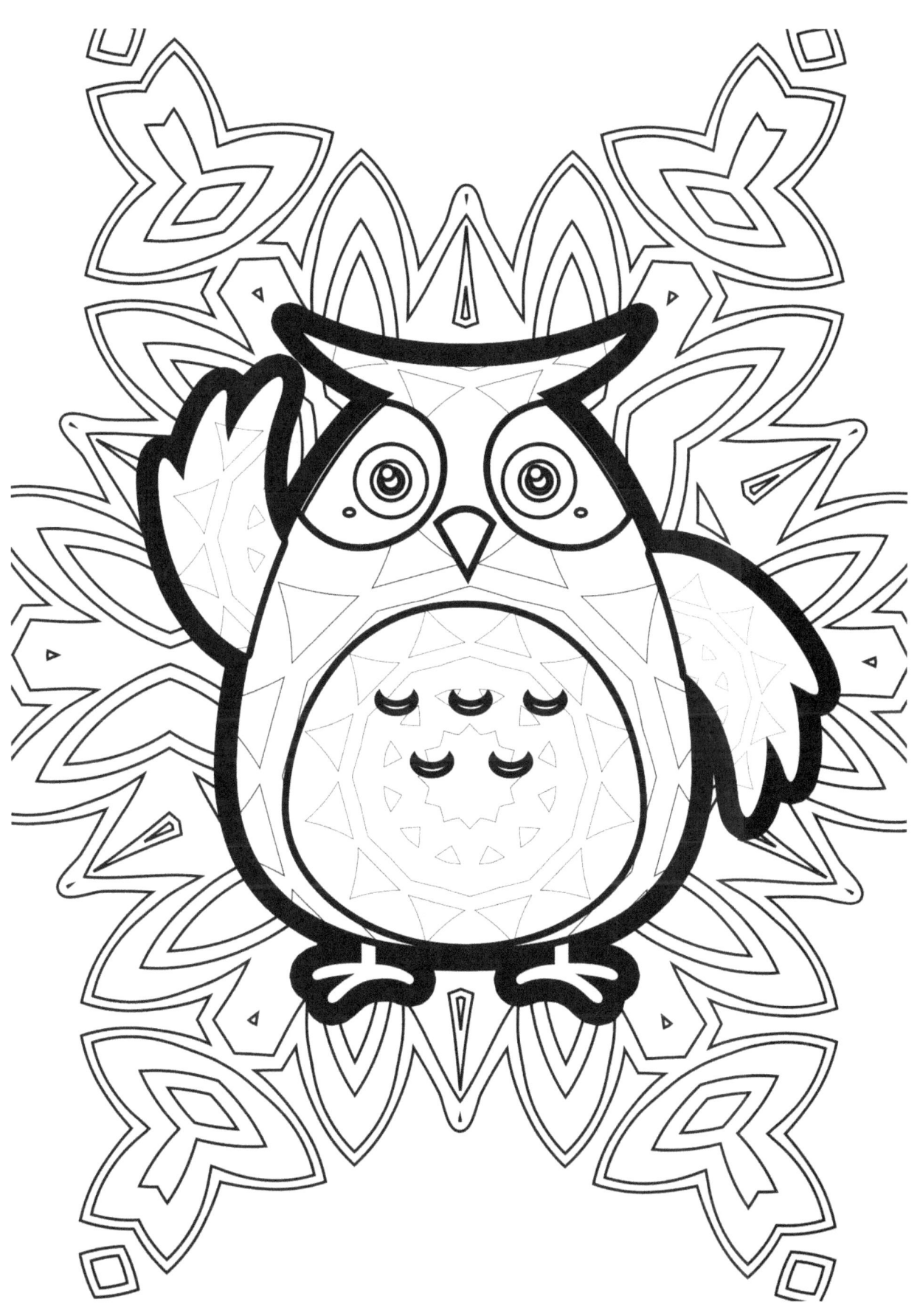

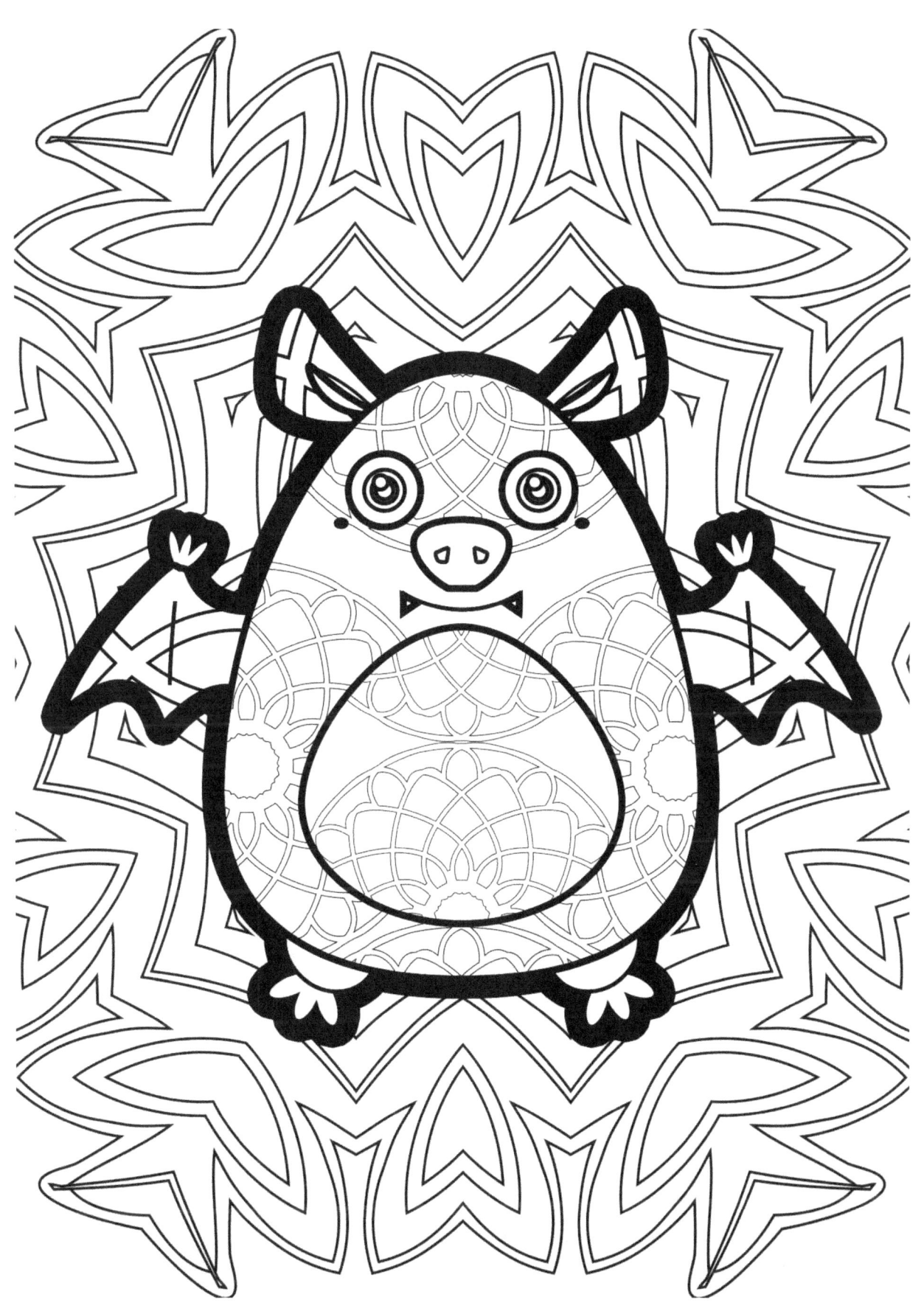

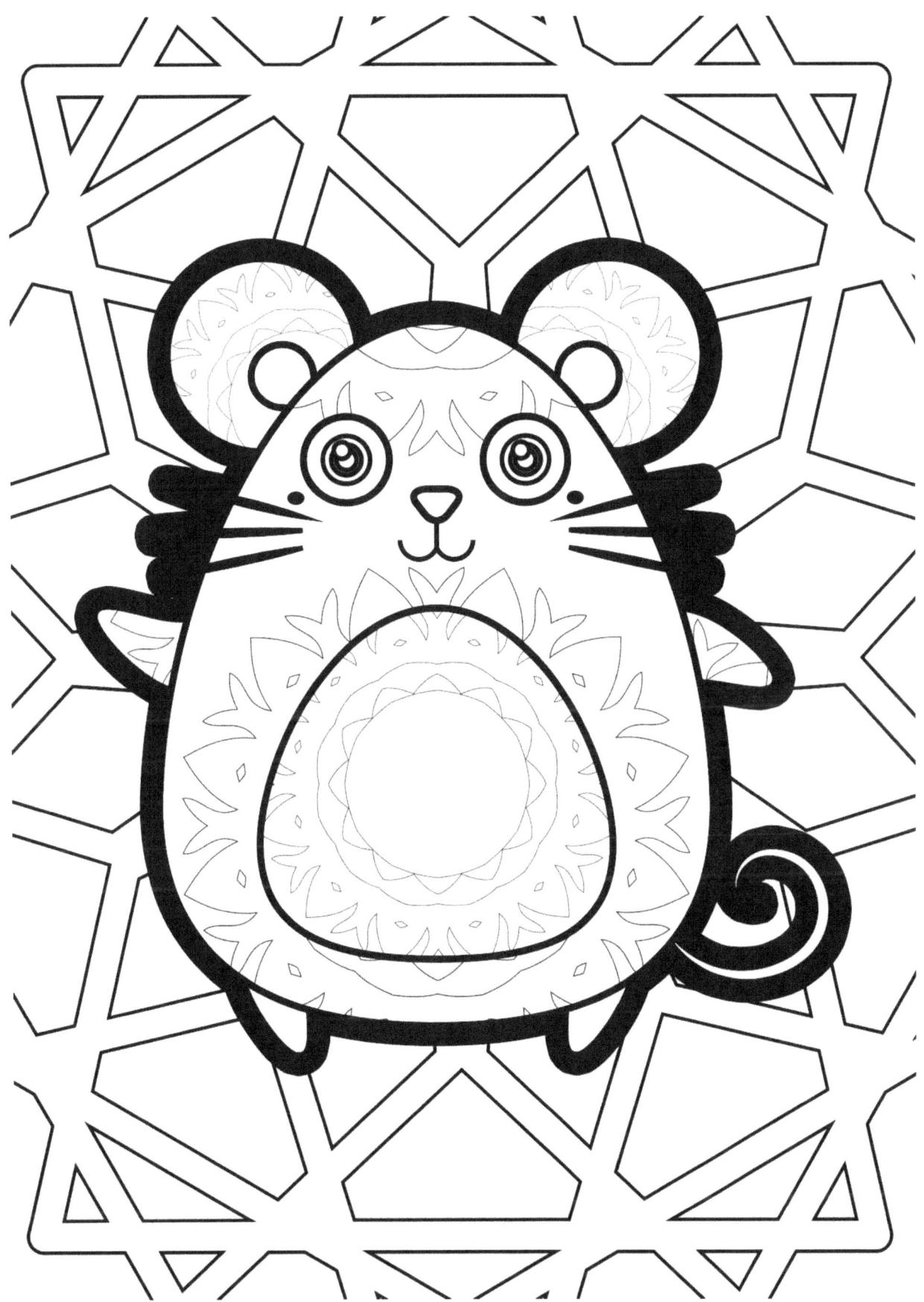

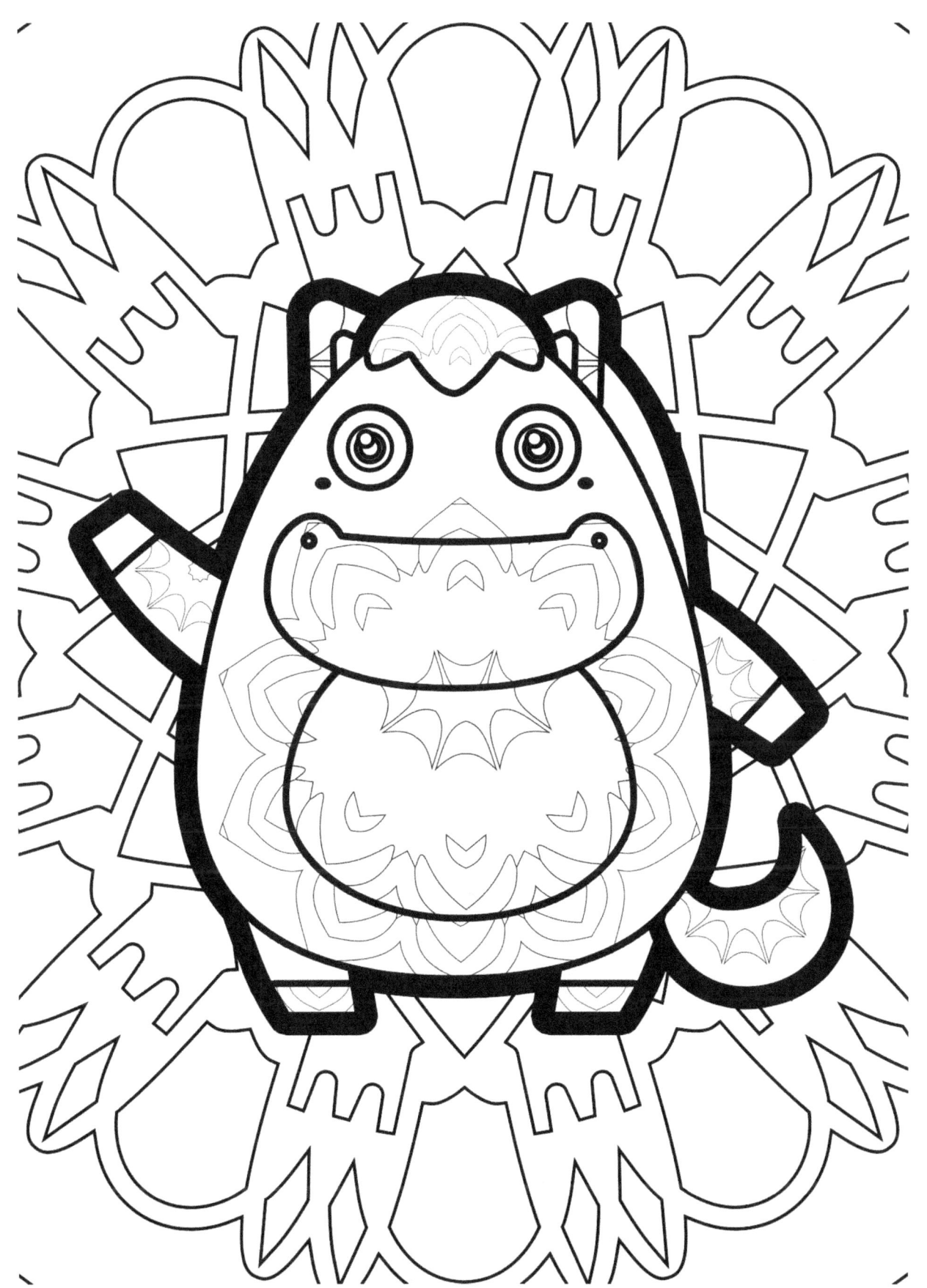

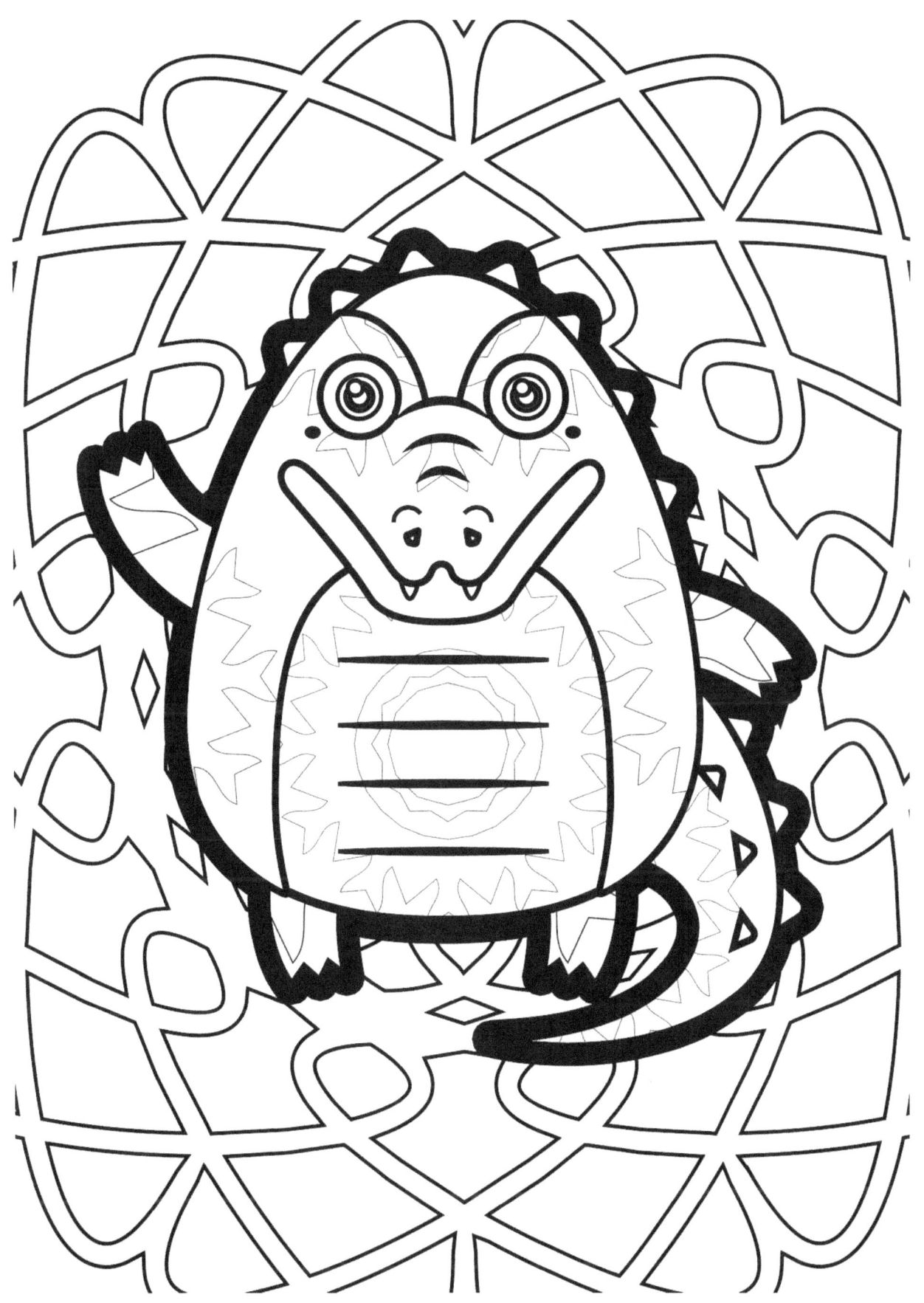

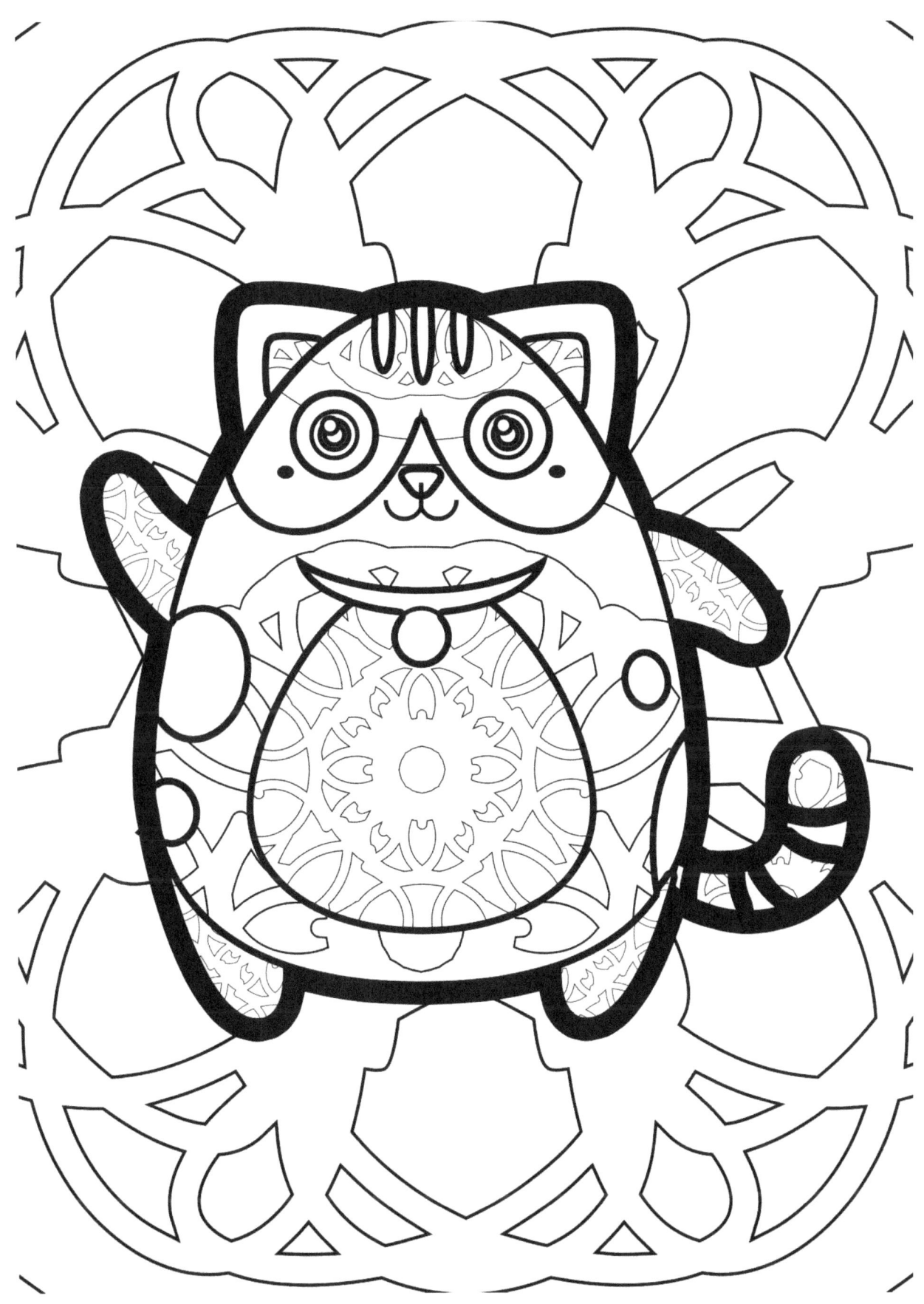

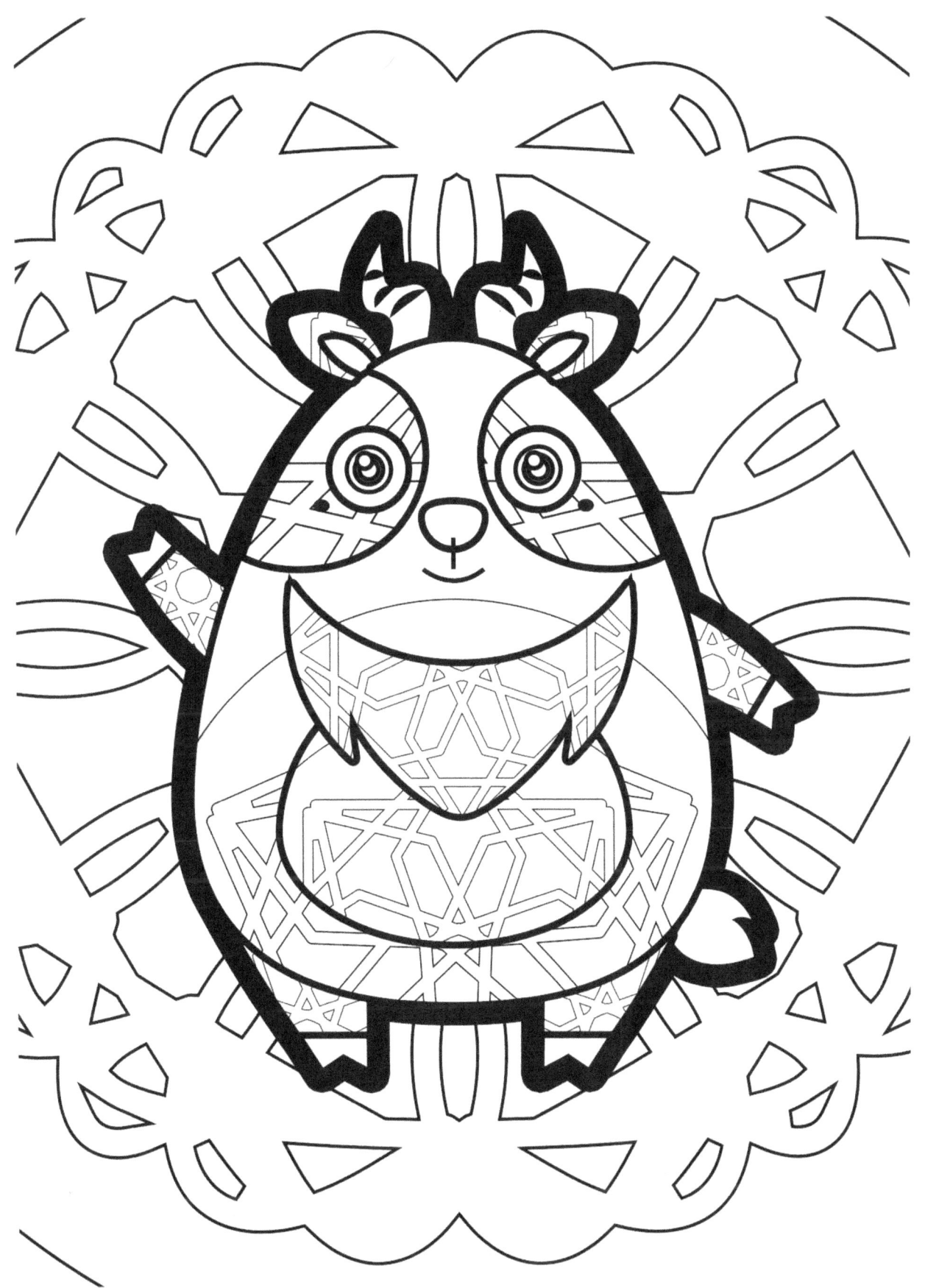

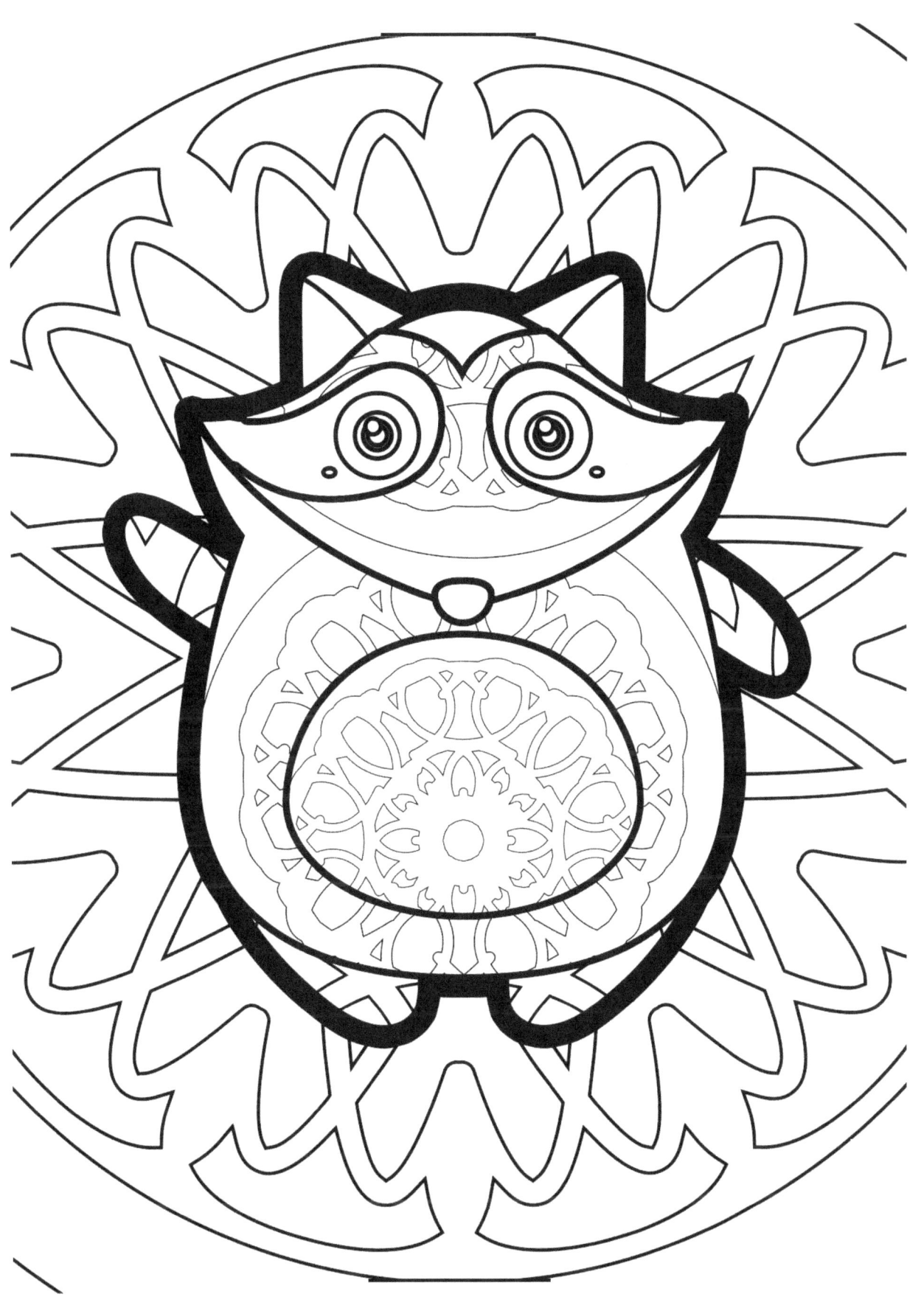

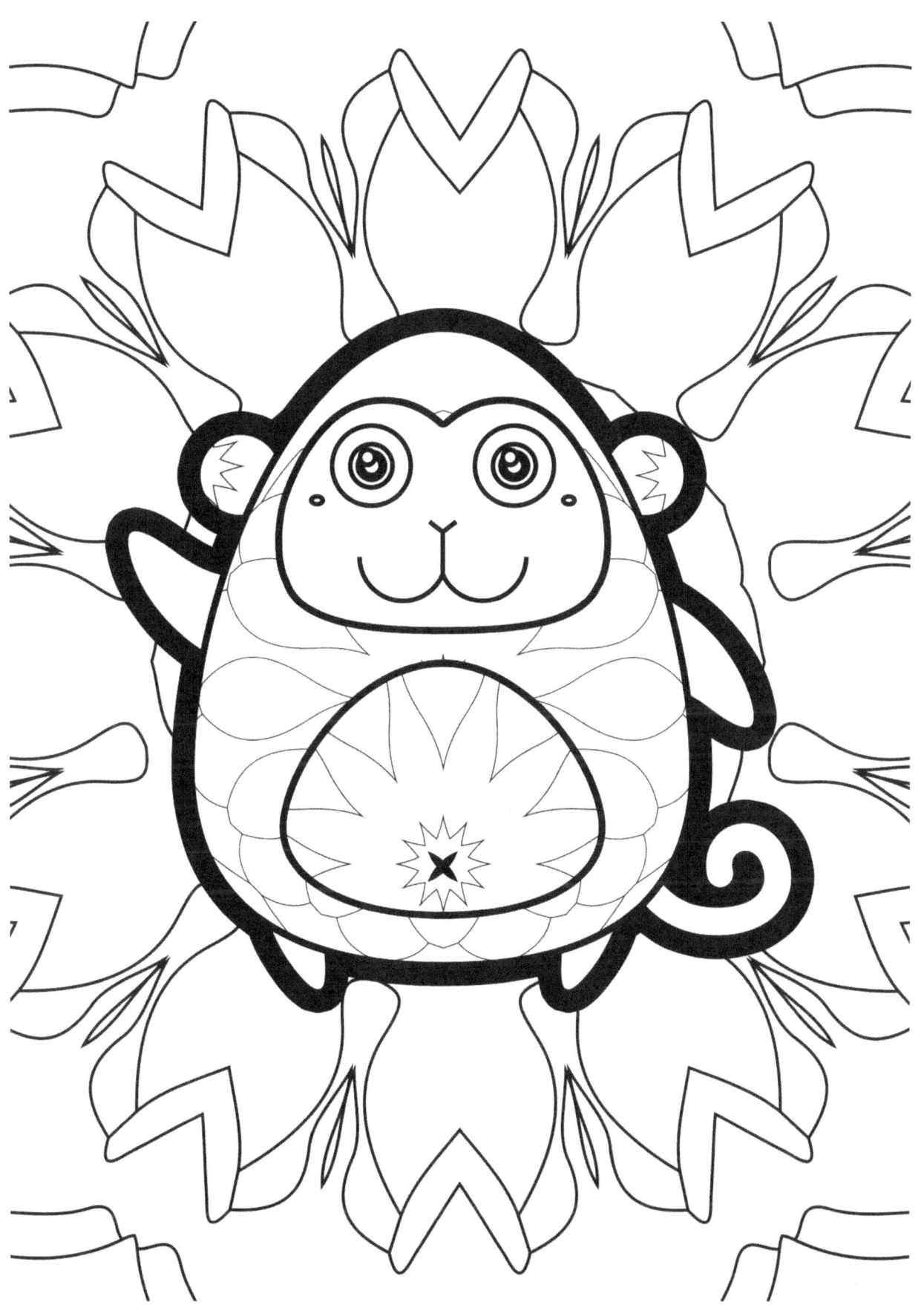

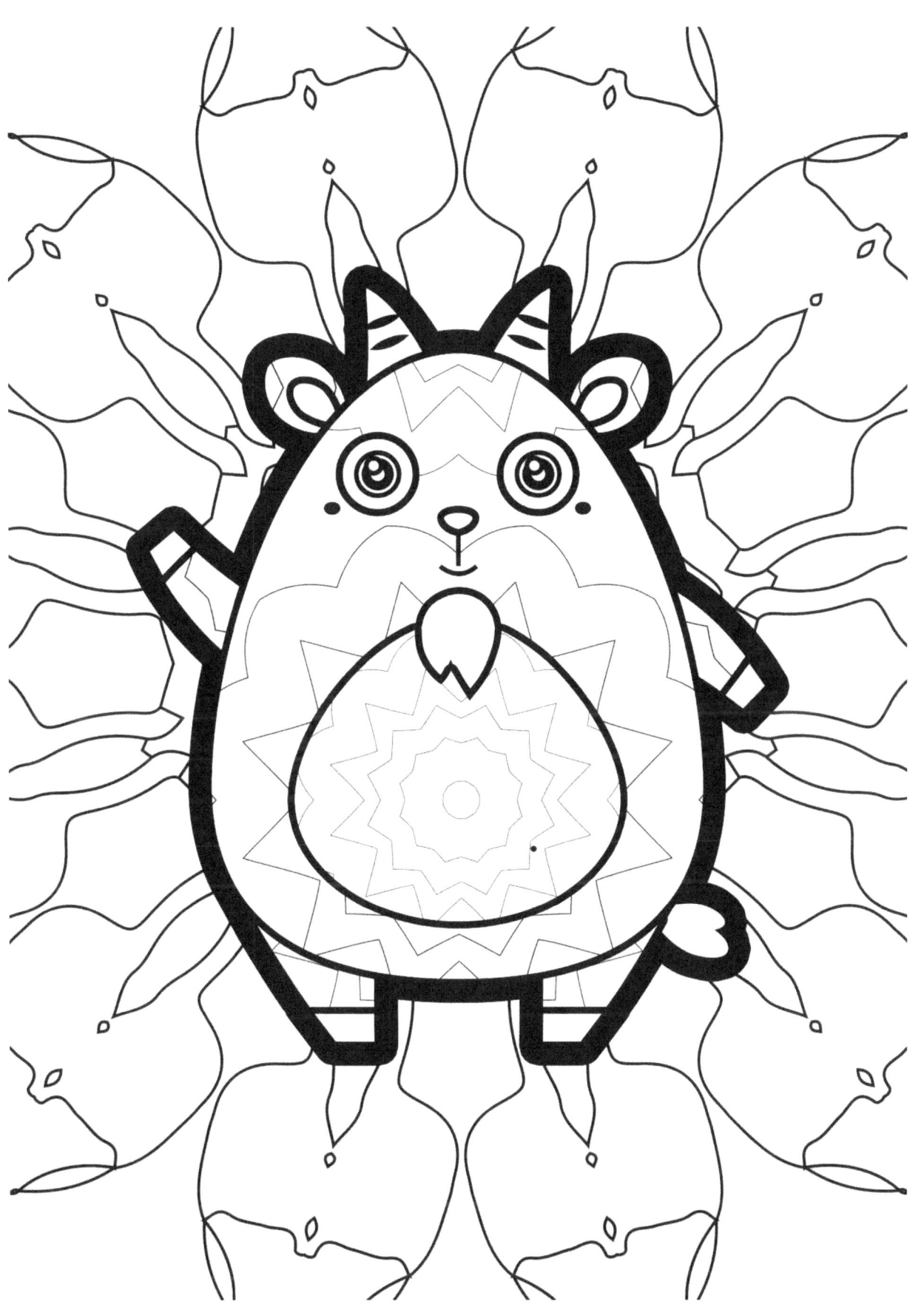

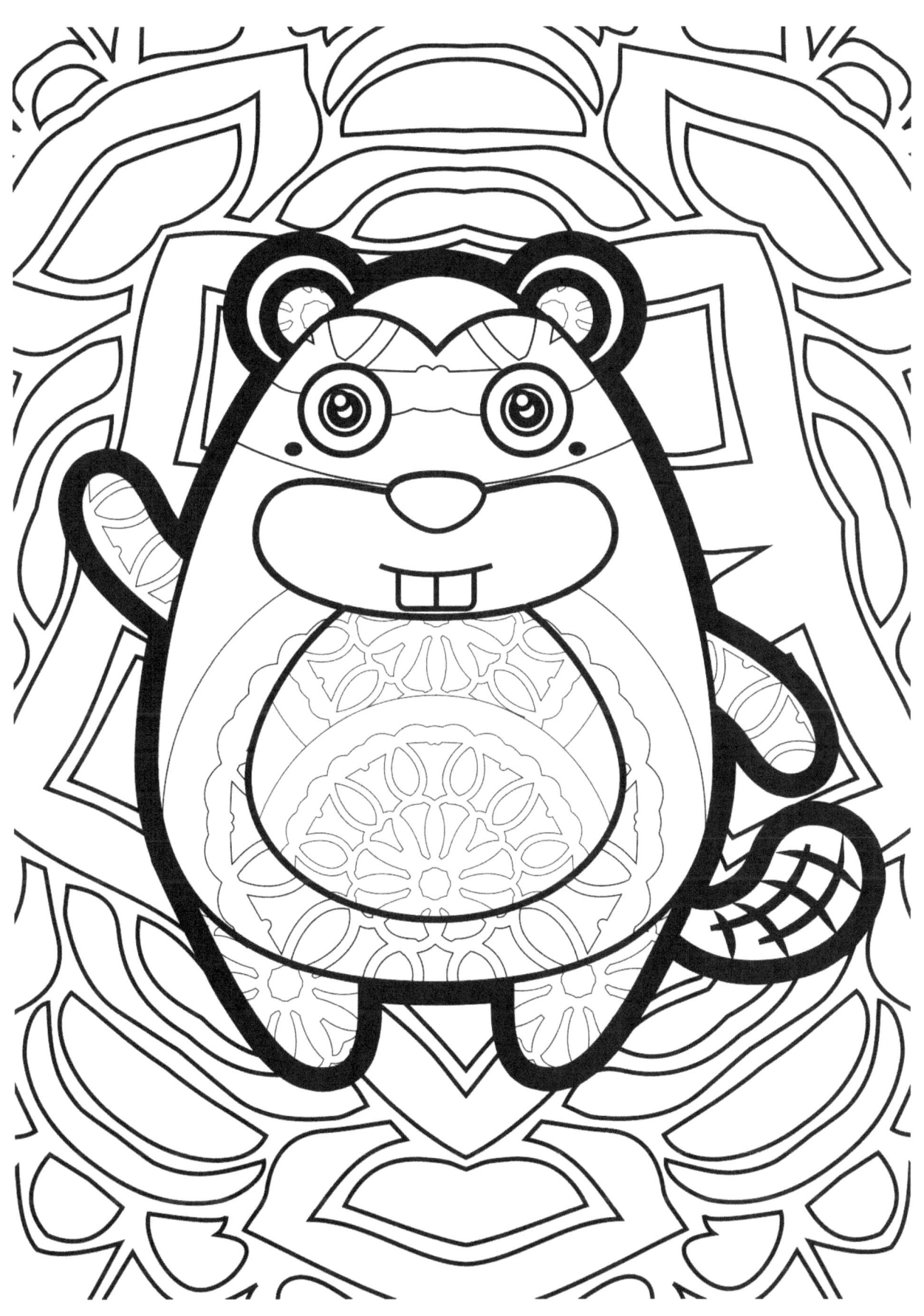

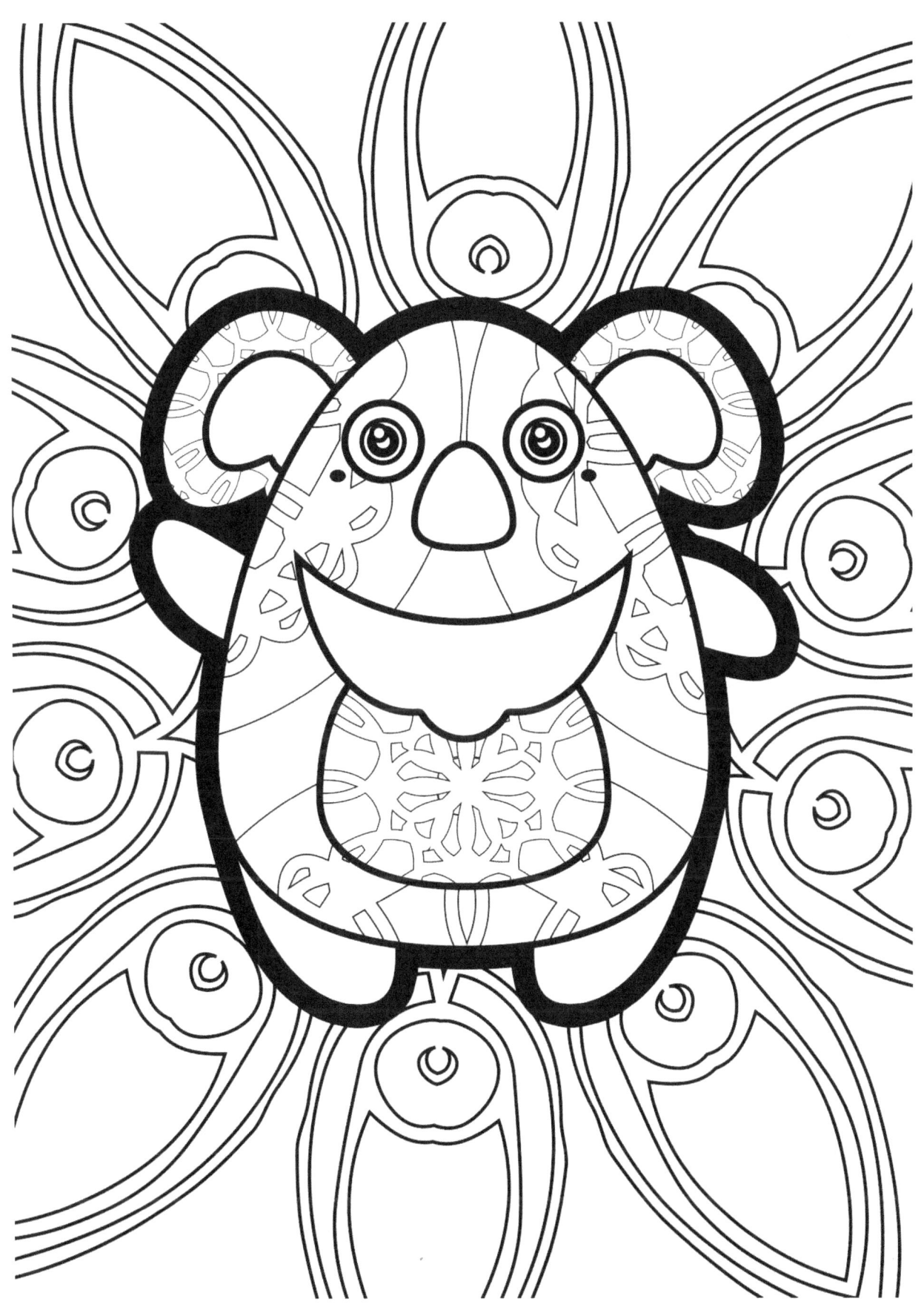

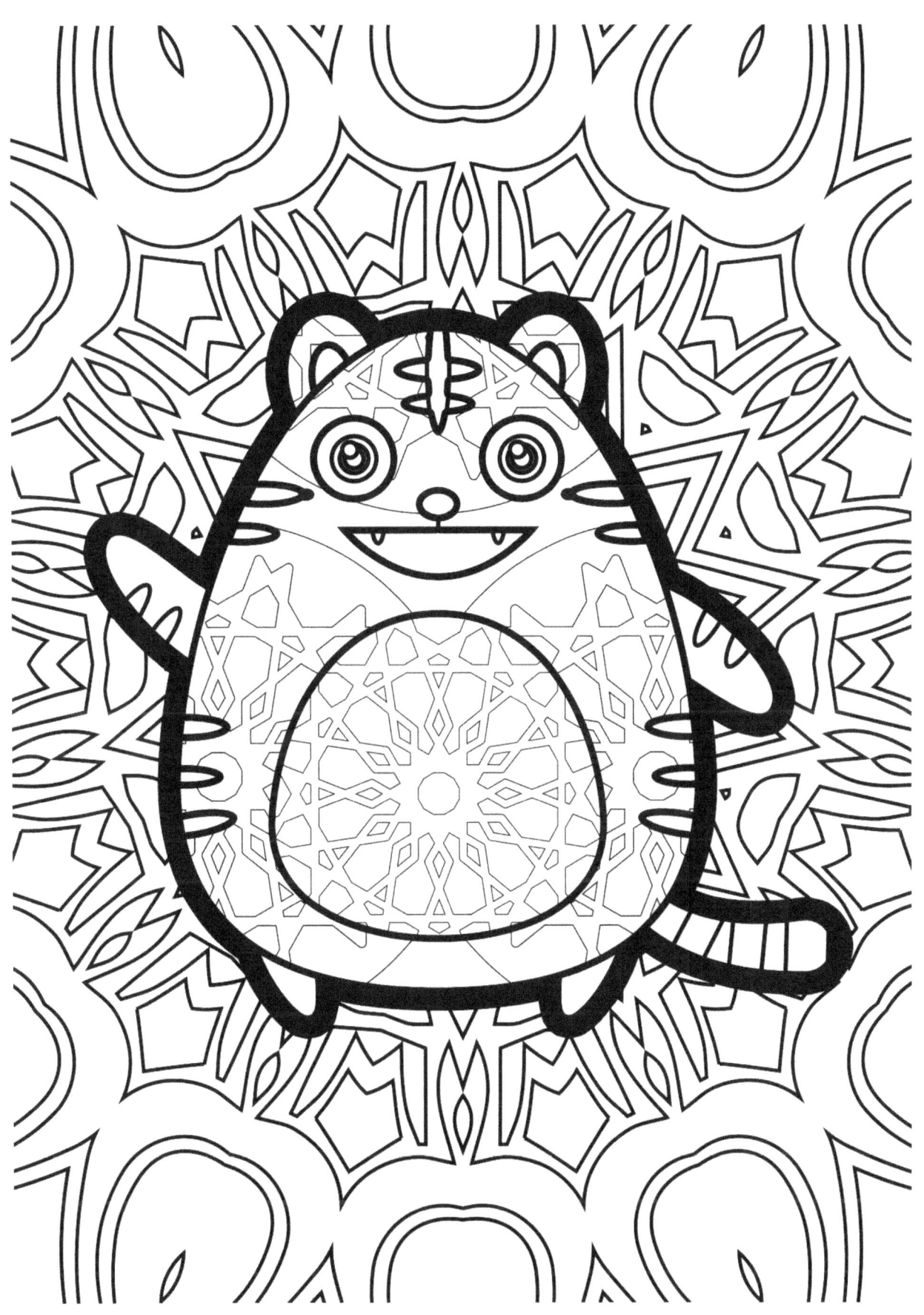

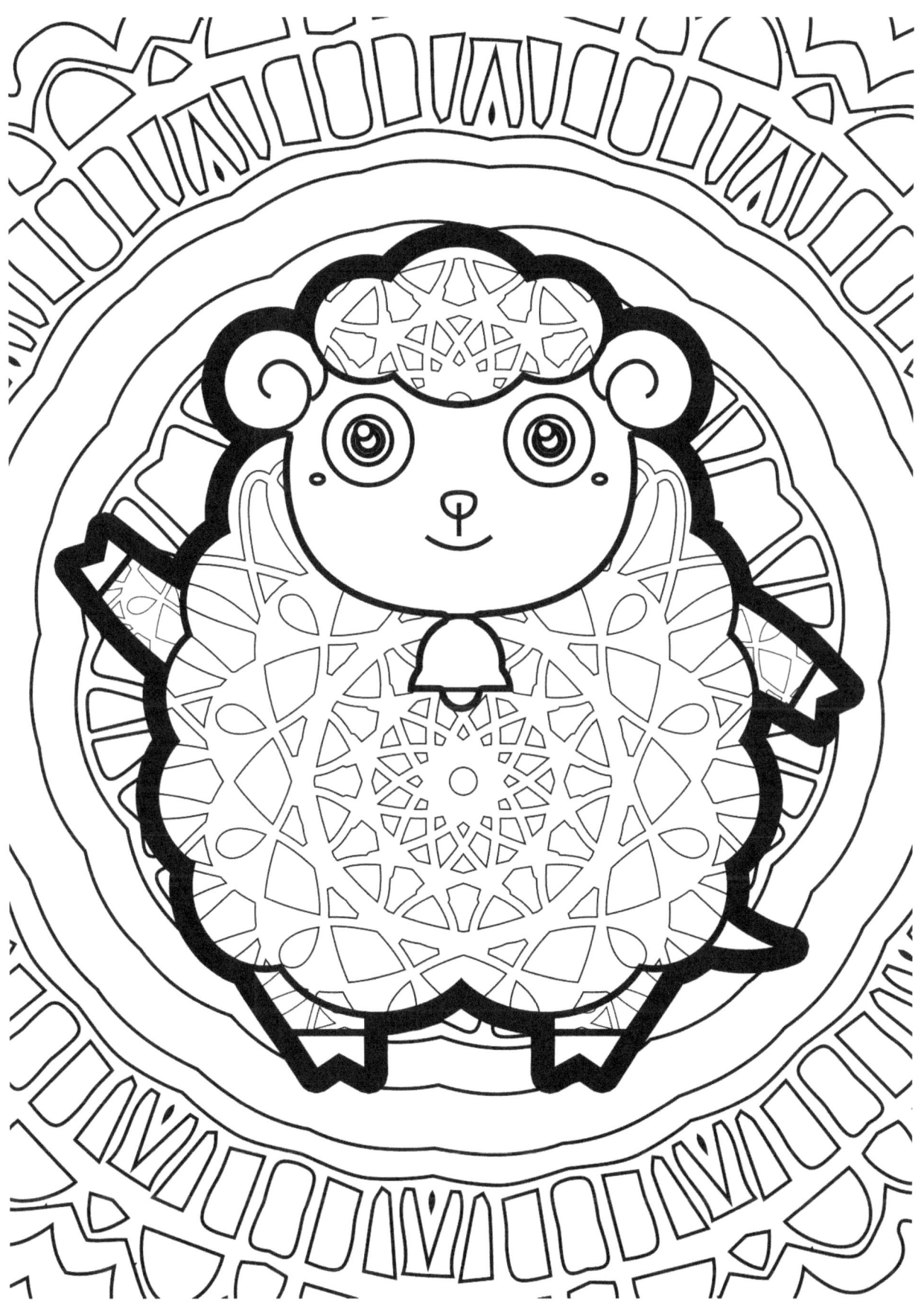

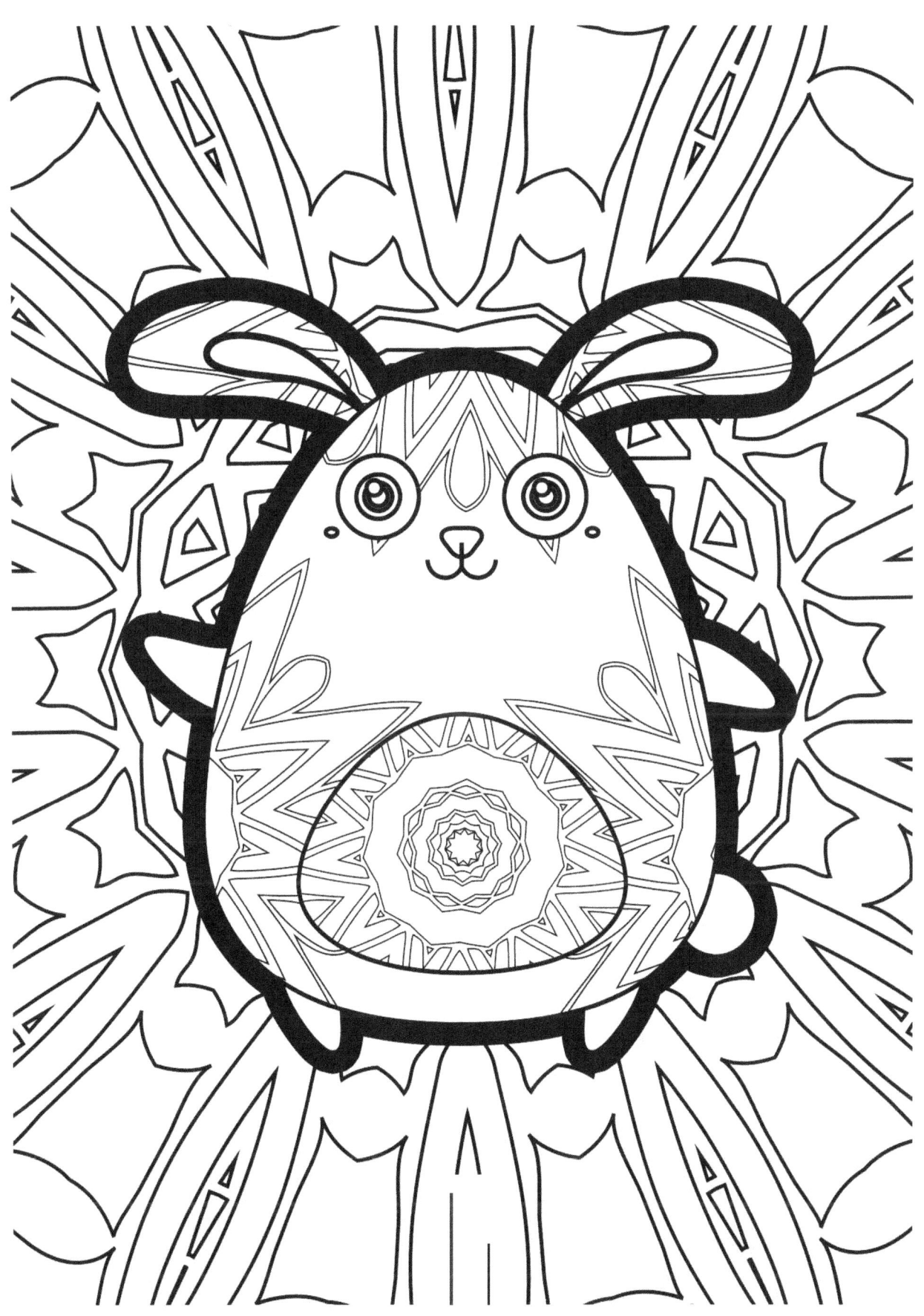

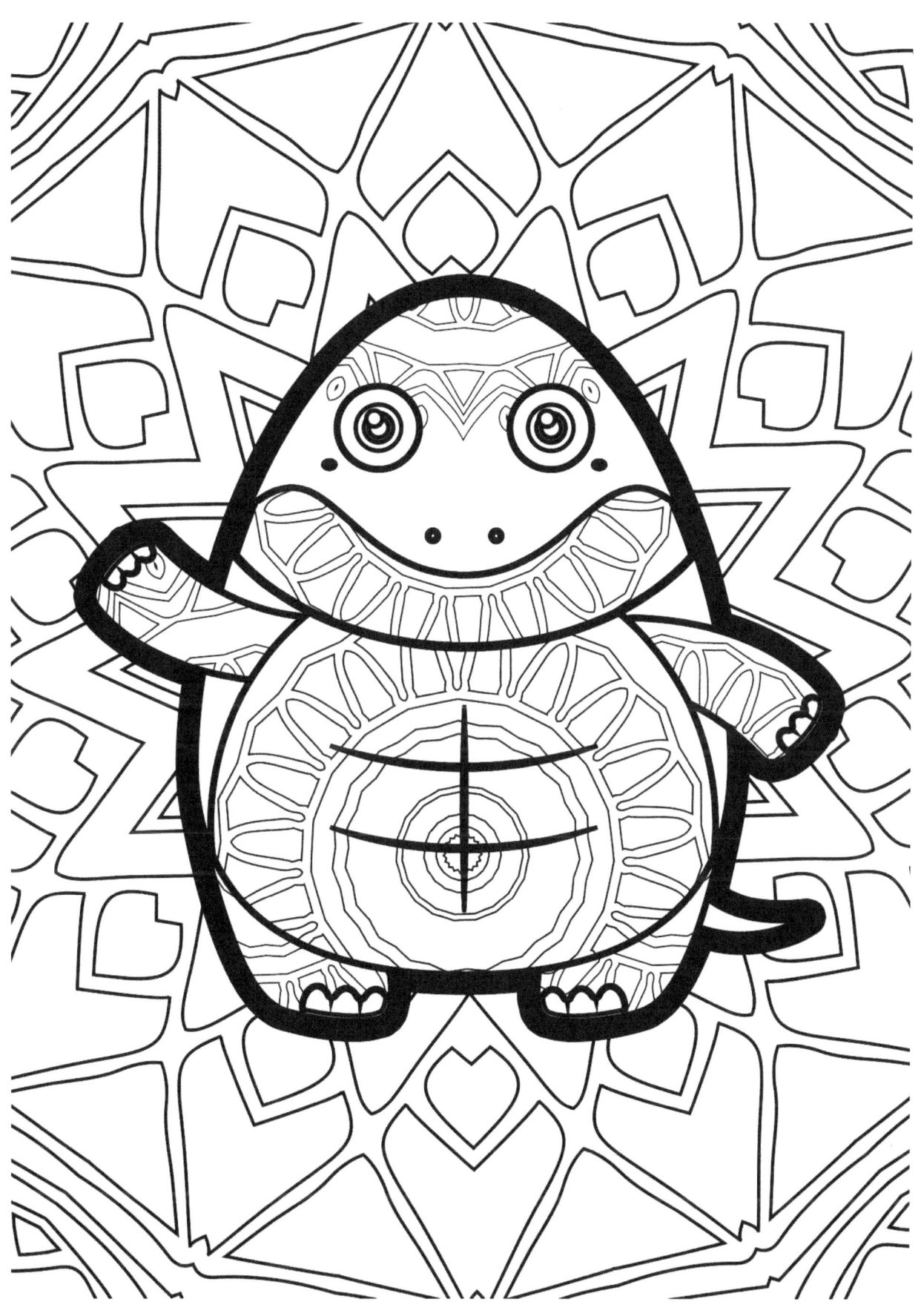

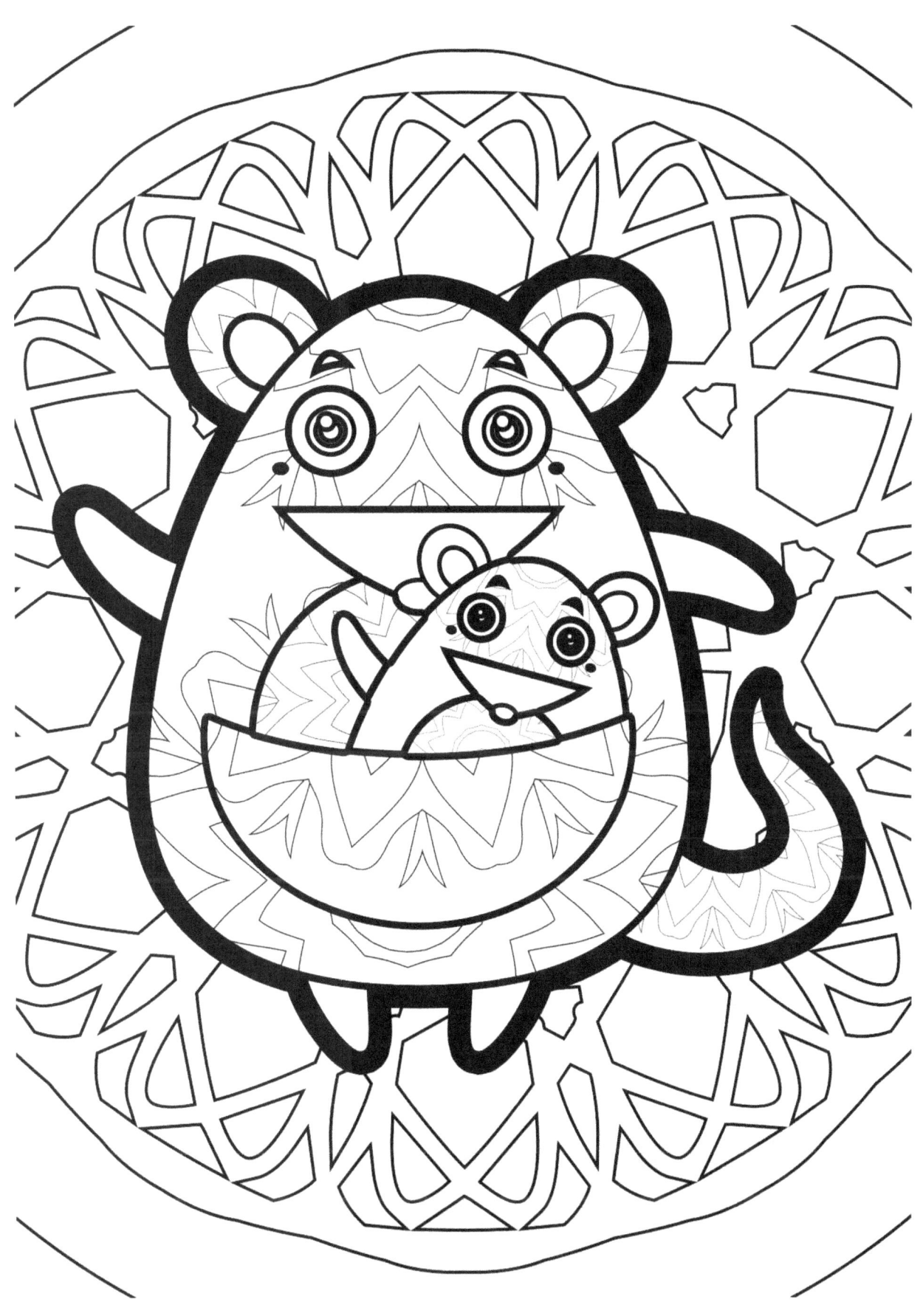

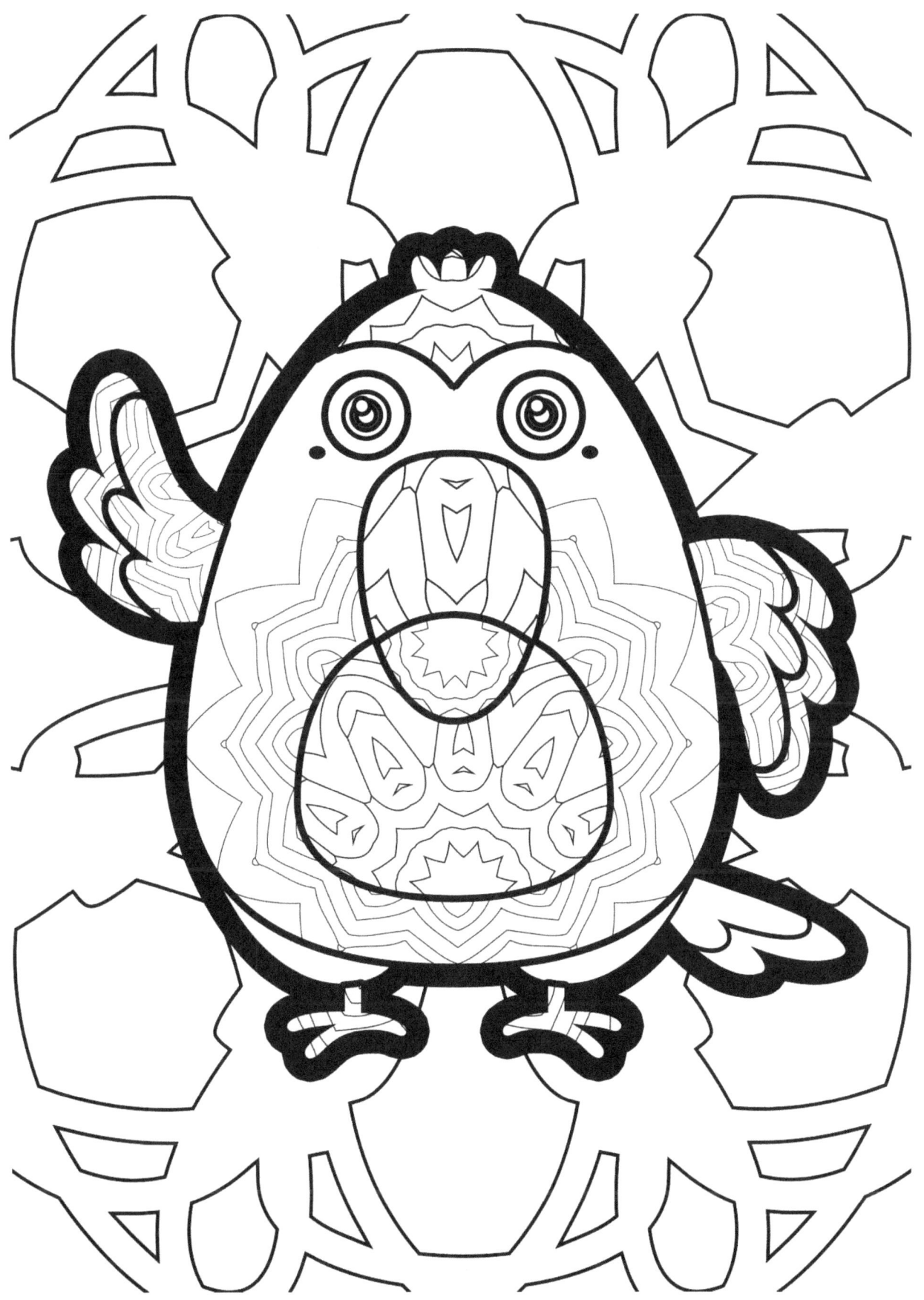

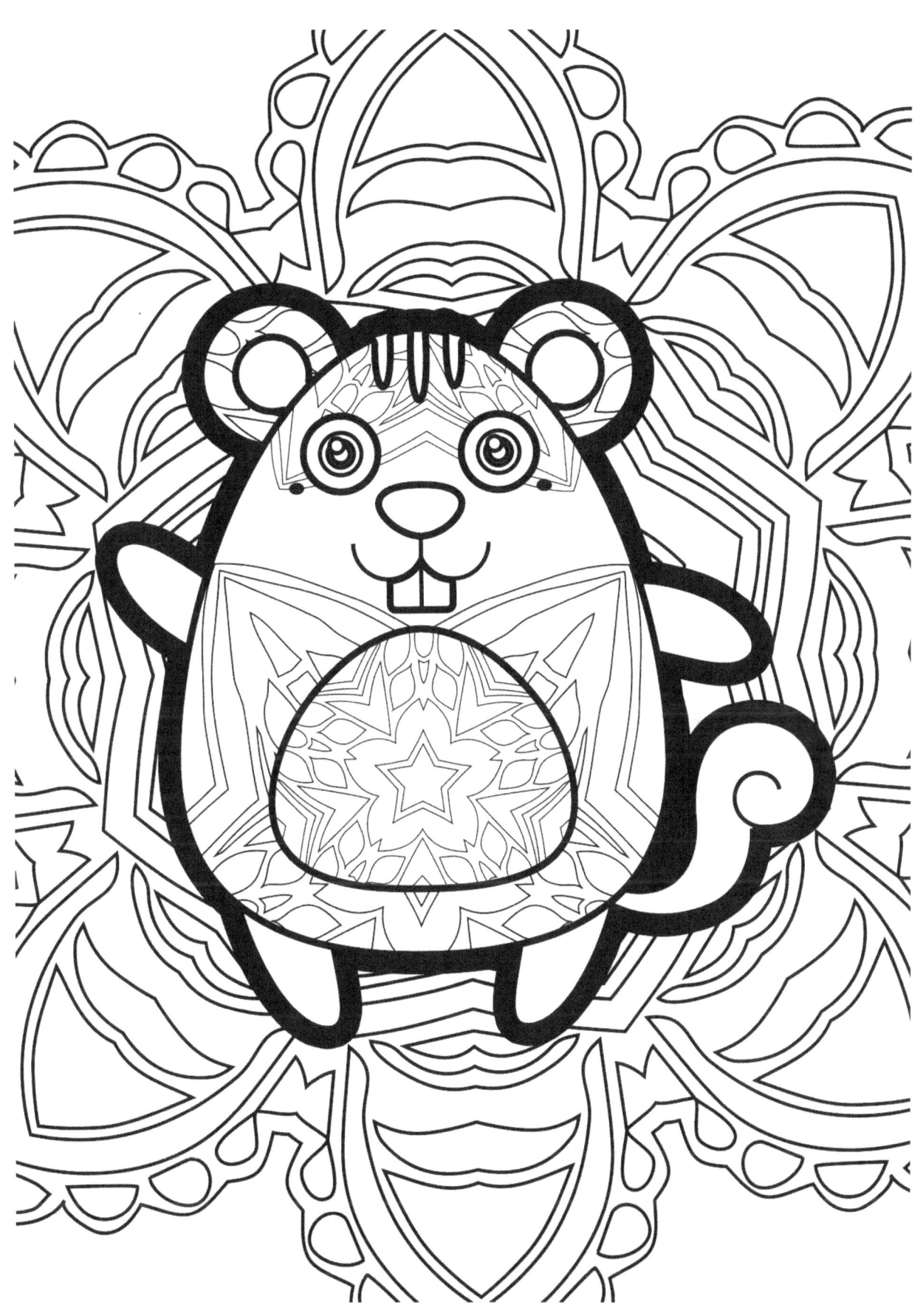

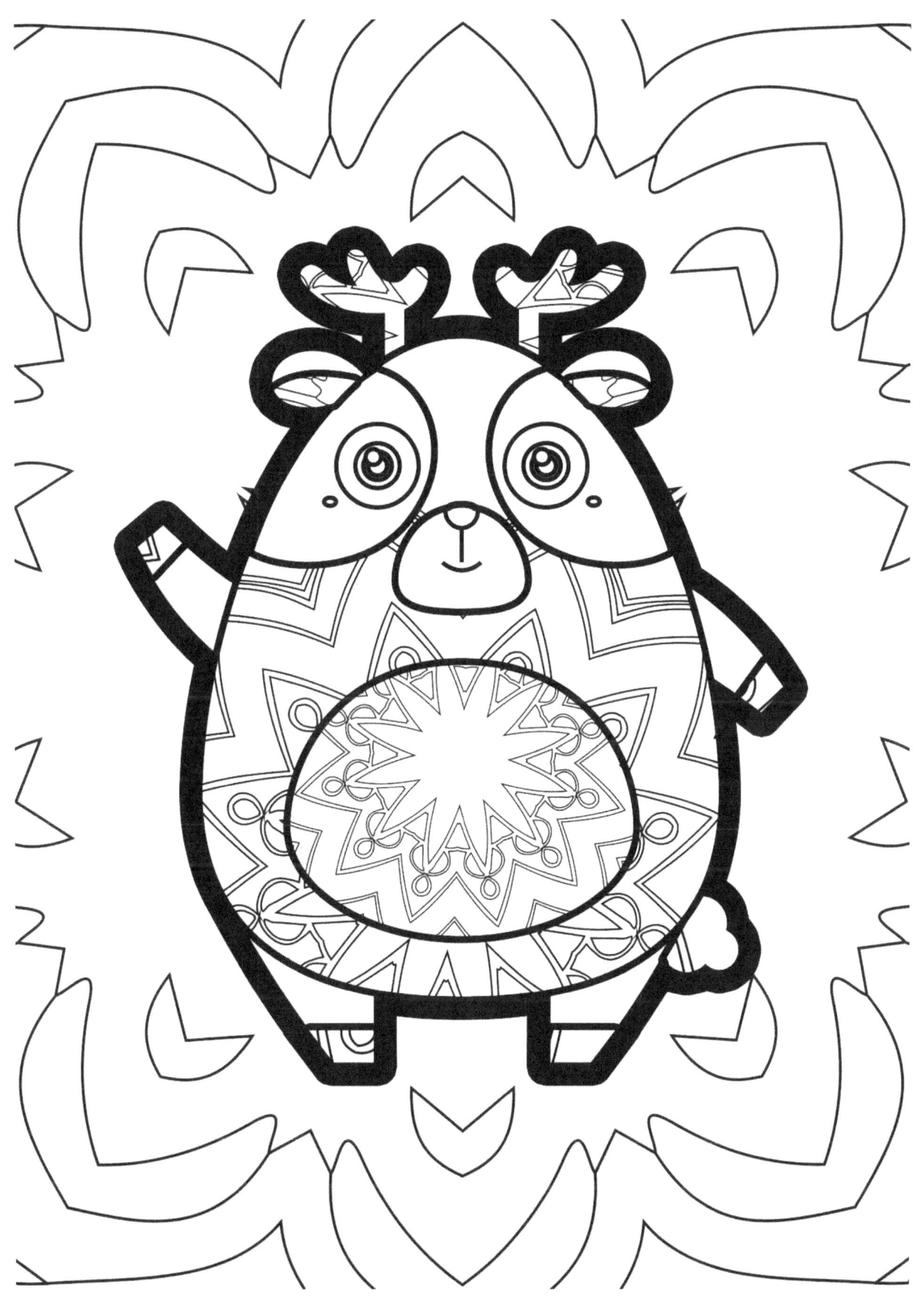

www.ingramcontent.com/pod-product-compliance
Lightning Source LLC
Chambersburg PA
CBHW081302180526
45170CB00007B/2531